broken and BEAUTIFUL

One Woman's Journey
through Clergy Sexual Abuse

Kristal Chalmers
with Eileen Peters

 FriesenPress

Suite 300 - 990 Fort St
Victoria, BC, V8V 3K2
Canada

www.friesenpress.com

Copyright © 2017 by Kristal Chalmers
First Edition — 2017

ISBN
978-1-5255-0945-2 (Hardcover)
978-1-5255-0946-9 (Paperback)
978-1-5255-0947-6 (eBook)

1. SELF-HELP, ABUSE

Distributed to the trade by The Ingram Book Company

Table of Contents

DEDICATION

The Japanese have an ancient tradition called kintsugi. Instead of discarding a beautiful bowl that has been broken, they use gold to repair it, creating a vessel that is unique and even more valuable. Kintsugi illustrates the truth that nothing is ever truly broken beyond repair. Rather than hiding the brokenness, the gold creates something new and cherished.

This book has been written for women who have experienced the shattering of their souls at the hands of someone they trusted as a representative of God.

Every story matters. Because for every story of brokenness the Master Potter waits to lovingly take the broken pieces and fashion them into something stronger and more beautiful than we would ever think possible. Our prayer is that this story may encourage you to allow Him to create something new and cherished out of your brokenness.

Kristal Chalmers

Eileen Peters

June, 2017

FOREWORD

My friend, Kristal Chalmers, is to be commended and applauded for the gracious resolve she demonstrates in documenting her difficult story. I say this because three decades as a pastor has frequently brought me face-to-face with the mult-faceted reality of sexual-abuse in religious circles. Accordingly, I am both grateful and confident that Kristal's work will serve as a voice for dozens of women I've encountered with similar painful experiences that, for various complicated reasons, will never be told in any public forum. Kristal speaks with prophetic clarity and compassion for a component of the Church community consisting of thousands who suffer in comparative silence.

I first encountered the many faces of sexual-abuse in evangelical Christian circles as a seminary student conducting research in 1983-84 for a major project. What I discovered shocked and horrified me. Bear in mind that those were years before headlines regarding pedophile Roman Catholic priests became all too frequent and before movies like *Spotlight* or TV shows such as *The Keepers* were on the public record. I quickly verified that not only did a sordid underworld of sexual impropriety exist in the evangelical sub-culture, but also that those aware of such certainly weren't talking about it.

Regrettably, yet thankfully, due to the bravery and determination of people like Greg and Kristal Chalmers and her parents, Lloyd and Eileen Peters, the man-hole cover obscuring the heinous reality of the many faces of sexual-abuse in religious communities is tenaciously being pried loose. On behalf of the dozens of victims, usually women or children, who have trusted me with their dark secrets over the thirty years of my pastoral career, I therefore thank them. The Bible makes no attempt whatsoever to avoid revelation or discussion of sexual indiscretion among the devout. In the service of credibility and integrity it is therefore long past time for the male-dominated Church environment to start paying greater attention to the implications of this truth.

Rev. Dr. Tim W. Callaway, Chair

MK Safety Net Canada

Personal names have been omitted to preserve anonymity. The initials AP stand for Associate Pastor.

INTRODUCTION

As I walked to the front of the stage, I was both nervous and excited. It was dark except for the white lights of the Christmas trees and the soft glow from the orchestra's music stands.

As a single low note curled through the auditorium, wrapping the audience in anticipation, my heart beat a little faster. The one plaintive note was answered by the piano and the rest of the strings as the lights began to come up. I took a deep breath and began to sing, "Love Incarnate, Love Divine …"

I felt overwhelmed as I sang the story of the Saviour's birth. In a crescendo of joy, the orchestra and the choir joined me as we sang together, "Noel, Noel! Come and see what God has done!"

But very few in that auditorium had any idea of the heart-shattering pain and betrayal I had walked through only two short Christmases before, when I was driving backroads looking for a cliff to hurtle over that would guarantee my death.

This is my terrible, beautiful story. And it is truly a story of "what God has done!"

I'm telling my story for one reason: I *know* that there are other stories like mine. Stories lived out quietly in the broken lives of women—and men— who have believed that they would have to carry their pain and their shame all alone.

Your story may not be exactly like mine, but shame is no respecter of persons. If you're reading this, there's a good chance that you, or someone you love, may be struggling to make sense out of feelings of guilt, betrayal, and loss. You may be angry or still in trauma. You may feel nothing.

This is not an easy story to tell. Common sense tells me that some who read this will write me off as an attention-getter. I also know there's potential for some that I deeply love to be hurt all over again. I've thought long and hard about telling my story, and I've sought advice from godly people whom I trust. As I've talked with more and more women who have suffered at the hands of a predator pastor, I've come to realize how fortunate I am to have a strong support system around me.

I'm also beginning to realize how determined many churches are to "keep the lid on" abuse in order to protect their reputation and guard against litigation. Although American courts are slowly beginning to view clergy sexual abuse as a criminal act, we in Canada are not even close to seeing this as an indictable offense. We're still having a hard time acknowledging that we even have a problem. Perhaps by telling my story, other victims who have been silenced will find the courage to come forward to tell their stories. As more stories are told, perhaps the church and denominational leaders will be forced to name what has been hidden for so long. As we gain strength, we will be able to walk together and care for one another, but most important of all ... the silence will be broken!

A friend with whom I shared the manuscript of this book has given me permission to quote from her email to me:

"Thanks for letting me read your book. It helped open my eyes to what happened in my own life years ago. Unfortunately, I think situations like this happen far too often, but it's comforting to know that you're not alone, and there is help available.

One of the things that stood out to me was how these situations start out. Little warning bells that I ignored, and situations that I felt uncomfortable in, but didn't know how to get out of. It was helpful to recognize these in my own life – and they won't happen again!

I will highly recommend this book!"

I know that if I had read someone else's story of clergy sexual abuse before experiencing it myself, I would have known to run for my life before the trap snapped shut. I pray this story will do that for someone else.

www.myvoiceback.com

CHAPTER ONE
What Is Clergy Sexual Abuse?

"Survivors of clergy abuse come from every walk of life and all religious traditions, (and) have some important traits in common, most notably the profound misfortune of crossing the path of a clergy person who is unable to set and maintain an appropriate boundary for the ministerial relationship." *1*

I don't remember a time when I didn't love to sing. My extended family on both sides is very musical, and there was always music in our home. To this day, family get-togethers always include lots of impromptu sing-alongs with music ranging from old, familiar hymns to favourite worship songs.

Before becoming pastors, my parents spent several years at a small Bible college where my dad was the Director of Music and my mom taught piano, so music was in my DNA.

When I was three years old, I prayed with my dad to accept Jesus as my Saviour, but my faith didn't really become my own until I was about fifteen. I was always tender towards the things of God and attended Sunday school every Sunday—which is pretty much expected when you're the pastor's kid! But a huge change in my life at the age of fourteen suddenly made me aware that I needed a real faith of my own.

My dad had accepted a call to pastor a church in a Chicago suburb, and that meant going from a school of 700 to one of 4,000. As I walked through the halls of my new high school, trying not to get lost, I felt like I'd been tossed into a foreign world. Those were lonely days, but it was during that time that I learned to lean on God in a way I never had before.

I was in college when I first realized that not only did I love to sing, but that singing actually made me feel alive. When I could use music to communicate truth, I knew I was discovering my purpose and passion. Soon I was asked to lead worship, and people began to affirm my gift with comments such as, "I was led into the presence of Jesus," and "Thank you for bringing me to a place of rest during worship this morning." I remembered reading that when your purpose and passion align, you find out why you were created. At the age of nineteen, I was pretty sure I had discovered my calling.

After graduating from college with my Bachelor of Biblical Studies, I was off to Anderson University to pursue a music degree. My brother was already there, studying to become a teacher. That year of sharing an apartment with my brother is filled with good memories— bringing a huge Christmas tree home on top of the car, sharing household duties, and getting to know one another as adults. Most importantly, I was exposed to a quality of music at the university that I hadn't experienced before. I had many opportunities to hear and study under skilled musicians who practiced their craft with excellence; however, the love of my life, whom I'd met in college, was living in Canada. We were married in 1999, and I moved to Canada. It was hard to move so far from home, and I struggled as a new bride.

In the middle of trying to find my way, we learned that a baby was on the way. While we had planned on raising a family, it was happening sooner than we'd expected, and I really thought my calling was over. I felt that with a new baby to focus on, my hopes of finishing my education were smashed. But as the months went by, I realized that motherhood was a priceless gift, and eventually I found myself once again trusting Jesus to have His way in my life.

We began attending a large church, and I became involved in the worship ministry. With the encouragement of senior staff, I began to grow as a worship leader. I realized that God had not forgotten the gifts and passion He'd placed in my heart, and I felt like I was "home."

Things were going well until we made the big decision to move back to the USA. Although I was excited to be close to my family, once again there were bumps in the road that made me wonder what God was up to.

I know now that He always has a plan, and He's *always* working out that plan! Even when He seemed silent and life felt confusing, I needed to trust Him with all of my dreams and goals. Once again, we found a wonderful church where I could be challenged and stretched as a musician and worship leader.

Unfortunately, in 2007 developments in the world of finance impacted not only our lives, but the lives of many Americans. As the economy began to crash, many people lost their jobs, homes, and in some cases, everything. We were one of the statistics. Although my husband was always one of the last to be let go, jobs became more and more scarce.

We were learning to lean on Jesus quite literally for our daily bread, but with three children and no quick turnaround forecast for the economy, we decided to accept an invitation from the church my dad was now pastoring back in Canada. We flew up to candidate, and as though God wanted to confirm that He was in this, my husband was offered four different jobs while we were there! We felt real peace that even though it would be excruciating to leave our home and friends, this was where God was leading us, so we packed everything up and headed north.

At the age of thirty-four I had landed my dream job. Even though it had felt like my dreams to lead a ministry of worship had stalled, and perhaps were finished, God was now reminding me that time means nothing to Him. He has a plan, and He is working out that plan!

My first week at the new job was so much fun—picking out office furniture, getting to know my computer, becoming familiar with the routines and the town. And then I met the associate pastor (AP). He had bought cell phones for the staff—all four of us. He didn't look me in the eye or say anything to me when he gave me mine, except something to the effect that we all shared group minutes, which was good because I was sure to go over on mine. He was so sarcastic that it threw me completely off guard. I didn't know what to think. This was the first time I had met him. Very quickly I learned to avoid him if I could, because one could never tell what kind of mood he was in. If his office door was closed, I would hesitate to knock. But there was much joy as I worked. I loved my job! Developing teams and pulling out talent in hidden places was so exciting. A worship culture was created, and people began to respond in ways that were meaningful.

Little did I know that within three short years, the dream would be destroyed by one man who was driven to satiate his need for power by controlling and crushing others who were vulnerable and easy targets. I would learn that I was not his first victim.

For Further Reading:

Clergy sexual misconduct, or clergy sexual abuse, may be a term you haven't heard before. Most women who have experienced it have never had a name for it. Often the inappropriate sexual behaviour of a minister towards someone in his church is labelled "an affair" or "adultery." It is neither.

Peter Rutter uses the term "sex in the forbidden zone" in his book by the same title to mean, "sexual behavior between a man and a woman who have a professional relationship based on trust, specifically when the man is the woman's doctor, psychotherapist, pastor, lawyer, teacher or workplace mentor." 2

Interestingly, a psychiatrist, doctor, school principal, or company CEO is held to a different standard than a minister. The courts are swift and concise in naming and prosecuting sexual behavior between a doctor and his patient. No one calls it an affair or tries to determine where the blame should be assigned. This is most often *not* the case in situations involving a minister and someone in his church. There are notable exceptions in Canada, but not many.

Patricia Liberty says, "Clergy sexual abuse is the misuse of power in a sexual way ... The sexual involvement of clergy with their congregation is not a "sexual sin" but an abuse of the power and authority of the pastoral office that is manifest in a sexual way." 3

The United Methodist Church has adopted this defi-
nition of clergy sexual misconduct: "…behavior of a
sexualized nature that betrays sacred trust, violates the
ministerial role, and exploits those who are vulnerable
in that relationship." They go on to say that sexual
abuse occurs when a person within a ministerial role
of leadership (lay or clergy, pastor, educator, counsellor, youth leader, or other position of leadership),
"engages in sexual contact or sexualized behavior with
a congregant, client, employee, student, staff member,
coworker, or volunteer."

Sexualized behaviour is that "which communicates
sexual interest and/or content. Examples include, but
are not limited to displaying sexually suggestive visual
materials; making sexual comments or innuendo about
one's own or another person's body; touching another
person's body; hair; or clothing; touching or rubbing
oneself in the presence of another person; kissing; and
sexual intercourse." 4

CHAPTER TWO
Groomed for Abuse

"The question keeps haunting me. When did it become sexual abuse? Was it when he encouraged me to become dependent on him? When he began sharing his personal problems with me? When he told me that we had a special and secret relationship and that no one had ever understood him as I did?" 5

THE ELDERS SOON DECIDED THAT SINCE MY DAD WAS the senior pastor, it would be in the best interest of the church to have me answer to the associate pastor. Since my dad and I are somewhat similar in personality, I thought a different perspective would be a good thing, so I readily agreed with the elders. Part of the associate pastor's job would now be to mentor me and the youth pastor and then later the children's director. I wonder now, based on his later assertion that "he had been in love with me for more than a year," and his previous actions with other women, what thoughts went through AP's head as he realized he would have carte blanche access to me at least once a week.

Although I was somewhat nervous to start with, we began meeting every Tuesday morning for an hour. I'd share what was going on in the Worship and Arts Department, and AP would encourage me, give some tips, and then pray for me and my ministry at the church. Most times I left those meetings feeling refreshed, because he seemed very encouraging … in fact, too encouraging sometimes. As time passed, he began telling me I was "too big for this town" and he hoped I wouldn't move away. I felt embarrassed but pleased that he thought I was doing a good job. He told me that I could get whatever I wanted … just like a cheerleader.

On the other hand, sometimes AP would make negative comments about what I was doing or how I was doing it, or he would relay a negative comment that someone else had said about me. Subsequently, I'd become discouraged and wonder why God had sent someone so inadequate to do this job. Sometimes AP would become so cold and nasty towards me that it would affect me greatly, but then he'd quickly become nice again. Soon I was trying to anticipate his moods. Much later he told me that he'd acted this way because he became jealous if others spent more time with me than he did.

Eventually I could walk into the office hallway and just tell what kind of mood AP was in and adjust my attitude accordingly. If he was happy, we were great buddies. If he was discouraged, I was the cheerleader. If he was mad, I made sure I was invisible. The staff was also familiar with his moods. It seemed like everyone walked on eggshells around him.

Overall, however, I felt that we were becoming good friends. AP also had a musical background, and we seemed to share a passion for raising the standard in our church. As the months rolled by, however, our meetings became more about what was happening in his personal life than about what was happening in my ministry. He'd sometimes cry and tell me that he felt he had no one to talk to. He seemed to be a troubled person, and I really wanted to help him. Looking back, I can't believe I was so stupid! He kept telling me that I couldn't share anything that was talked about in our meetings, so I just kept trying to help him. One time I referred to something we had discussed (work related) that I had inadvertently shared with the senior pastor who was my dad. AP became extremely angry. I got sick to my stomach, feeling like I'd betrayed him, but not understanding why it was such a big deal. After that episode, I went to great lengths to assure him that I was a safe person and would keep things confidential.

My grandmother had come to live with my parents at that time, and one of the joys of living so close was being able to share laughs and love with her. My children also had the privilege of getting to know her well.

Grandma had been in a near-fatal accident a few years before, and it was hard to see the vivacious grandmother with whom I'd grown up struggle with her injuries. After some years of struggling, we knew the end was finally coming. One day while driving to work, I just felt like I needed to drive to see her instead, so I walked into her room and knelt beside her bed. She had stopped eating and we were told that within the week she would likely be gone. I held her hand and cried. Her hand was so soft and worn. It was a holy moment.

She loved life. She loved me. I know she prayed for me. She celebrated with me. She was authentic and messy, and she was stubborn! I remember one day I wheeled her chair into the piano room and convinced her to play some old hymns. She could turn anything into a polka!

As I knelt beside the bed that day, I keenly felt the depth of what I was losing. I kissed her and went to work. A few days later, we gathered by her bed and watched her take her final breath. There was a moment where, I promise you, the angels were hovering excitedly, waiting for this saint to join the party! I'm so glad I was there to say good-bye.

Everyone was kind, but when I told AP, he took me in his arms and cupped my head in his hands and hugged me. I cringed inside, because it felt intimate and weird, but once again I felt like I was overreacting, so I dismissed it. Little did I know that every time I shut down these internal "checks," I was giving my abuser more power.

For Further Reading:

"Grooming is a process whereby the religious leader breaks down a woman's defenses, making her feel special, perhaps pointing out her spiritual gifts, or in another way using his position as a religious leader to develop a close relationship and isolate her from others. He uses personal warmth to obscure what his true intention is. According to Patrick Carnes, some of the ways this warmth is expressed include: expressing admiration, caring, and concern; indicating that he looks forward to a long-term relationship with her; making affectionate gestures and touching; talking about a shared project; complimenting and sharing personally in ways that are inappropriate for a relationship between a religious leader and parishioner, student, or employee (Carnes, 1997). He co-opts religious and spiritual language into an agenda designed to meet his own needs.

"It is a gradual and subtle process, and one that has extraordinary power, desensitizing her to increasingly inappropriate behavior while rewarding the victim for tolerance of that behavior. He speaks for God, saying things like, 'You are an answer to my prayer. I asked God for someone who can share my deepest thoughts, prayers, and needs and He sent me you;' and "God brought us together because He knew how much I needed someone like you." (Liberty, 2001, p. 85). Later, she may find it trite and feel humiliated that she believed him, but at the time, it is a powerful way to exploit her and silence her doubts, throwing off her inner moral compass (Liberty, 2001). After all, spiritual leaders are expected to act in one's best interests, and he is capitalizing on any vulnerabilities he has found in her to exploit. Frequently he is describing his own marriage as unfulfilling.

"Grooming is essentially seduction in a relationship in which he holds spiritual power over her. He provides a story, or what Carnes calls a 'sustaining fantasy or supportive script' (p. 56) that justifies the relationship. He may be doing wonderful things in ministry and needs her support for his calling. For example, the alleged story of evangelist Jim Bakker is that he used his role as a tired minister to millions of persons while no one ministered to him as a means of gaining sexual access to women, almost as though that by giving to him sexually, they could empower him to minister to others (Friberg & Laaser, 1998).

"There may be some shared mission, a cause for which they need to partner. She senses something is not quite right, but it is a relationship she has been taught to trust—he is a spiritual leader, after all—so she allows him to say and do things she would not allow a man to do in a normal friendship. At the same time, she becomes increasingly anxious. Anxiety escalates physiological sexual attraction and arousal (Carnes, 1997), therefore intensifying the bond between them. Clergy have organizationally sanctioned easy access to intimate settings under profoundly intimate circumstances.

They are permitted an instant intimacy not normally granted to other people in society.

We tend to follow a spiritual leader's lead and trust. If a minister invites someone seeking counseling into the office and closes the door, she will most likely assume it is always done this way and see nothing wrong with it. Most of the time, we are indeed in good hands and safe. But if the minister is steering toward a sexual relationship, the congregant would have a hard time figuring that out and stopping him. She simply has less ability to say no and more reason to comply with his wishes—she is vulnerable (Horst, 2000).

"With that kind of trust, he can easily minimize her concerns and doubts about the appropriateness of their relationship, slowly nudging at and then crossing her sexual boundaries (Fortune, 1999). The first boundary crossings may be covered on his part by claiming lack of intention. For example, if he hugs her or touches her in a way that is just slightly over the edge of appropriate-ness, she may question her own ability to discern what happened. If she does question or confront him, he may say, 'I was just trying to comfort you' or 'I was just communicating how dear our friendship is' (Carnes, 1997). As a consequence, she may berate herself and actually feel embarrassed at having questioned his intentions: 'I should have known he was just being caring; how could I be so overly sensitive?' Because of the unusual level of trust that women place in religious leaders, perpetrators are able to deprive their victims of their usual resources for discernment, good judgment, and action. The more subtle the coercion, the more invisible the power play and the greater the damage done to her (Horst, 2000).

"She blames herself rather than seeing his use of his role as spiritual leader to manipulate her to allow him intimacy she would never allow another man outside of her marriage. The first actions seem small; how could a victim tell someone about the pastor holding her hand in both of his in prayer without sounding that she was sexualizing a small act that he intended as comfort?

"As one client said, 'Compared to him, who was I?' Women often justifiably believe that no one will believe them. The church deacons or the dean of the seminary may believe the woman "asked for it," or that she tempted him. Others may well believe that she was dressed inappropriately or somehow was sending him signals. Indeed, she may even on some level have wanted him to be attracted to her. She may have been lonely and found him attractive. But that does not excuse his behavior or condemn her feelings. She trusted him to be the safe spiritual leader.

Eventually his behavior becomes overtly sexual, and she has to decide what to do. But she very likely has no one to turn to but the perpetrator himself to sort out her confusion. If she confronts him, he may apologize profusely, minimize what happened, back up in the grooming process, and wait until she has once again placed trust in him. Victims often question their own stories, wondering if they remember events correctly, or if they are making too much out of what may be the first forays across her sexual boundaries. What she does not realize is that she is already caught by the secrecy. If she tells anyone at this point, she might not be believed, or she might be labeled a seductress. If she does not tell anyone, he will continue to cross her boundaries and, later, others will question why she did not 'do something' sooner. There is no way out at this point that does not shame her, even if she wants out. Whatever she is feeling, she is confused, sometimes on one level enjoying the attention and affection she is receiving from him, making it even more impossible to escape, even though she is alarmed and frightened. These emotions deepen the attachment—he is the only one with whom she can discuss her feelings." 6

CHAPTER THREE
Understanding Power

"Powerful people have a lot to lose—a lot of power, that is. So they intimidate through fear, surrounding themselves with other powerful people. Strangely, spiritual leaders deny their power—that's what makes everything so convoluted. Just understanding this has a way of lessening the blow to survivors." 7

A YEAR AFTER WE STARTED MEETING, AP AND HIS WIFE gave me a birthday card that had a princess button on it. He'd already started making comments about how I was the princess and always got what I wanted. That stung at first and made me feel like a stupid teenager trying to pretend that I fit in, but I accepted it as his style of humour and chose to ignore it. He said that I was a flirty cheerleader who got everyone around me to do what I wanted. His tone of voice was strange, and I began to wonder if he was jealous of what I did, but I dismissed that thought immediately. He was well known in the community and loved by everyone in the church ... or so I thought. Also, it seemed like he was in charge of a lot of things in the church, because he had been at that church for so many years. He was more than twenty years into full time ministry— of course he wouldn't be jealous of me!

At the same time, he'd say things like, "Please don't leave. I'm so scared you're going to go get hired by some big church, and you'll be gone." I thought that was ludicrous for many reasons. My parents were here. My husband was happy with his job, and this move had been so traumatic for our oldest child. I wasn't looking for another move any time soon. I would assure him I was there to stay. I loved my job. He was the only hiccup in it, and when he was nice, he was very, very nice. I focused on that.

Two years into my job, the church decided to send the staff and their spouses to Atlanta for a conference. One day in our meeting, AP said, "I wish it was just us going to Atlanta." The first time he said it, I assumed he meant just my husband and me, along with him and his wife. The next time he said it, I was afraid of what his answer might be, so I never asked him to clarify. In Atlanta, he seemed moody most of the time, and I was glad when the conference ended and we could all go home.

Nothing more was mentioned after our return from Atlanta, but by now I was beginning to feel like I was his full-time counsellor. It seemed we hardly ever got around to talking about worship arts. He always steered the conversation in a personal direction.

I began to feel like AP was treating me as if I was his equal, and that confused me. I was concerned sometimes that I wasn't respecting AP as my mentor, and I'd say things to that effect. But he told me that wasn't a problem.

Life got back to normal after Grandma was gone, and we got into full swing planning for the seventy-fifth anniversary of the church. By this time, our Tuesday meetings often included AP crying over painful memories of his past, and sometimes me praying for him. Often on Sunday mornings I would get to the church early to go over music. AP would come over to the piano and tell me how beautiful I looked. Since he was so much older than I, I didn't think anything of it. I thought he was just being nice. After all, his wife was slim and cute and they seemed like a perfect couple. So often I felt like an ugly duckling.

It was during this time that he admitted to being jealous of all the people who came into my office, so I tried to meet people outside of my office. That seems so crazy when I think about it now! He even said he was a bit jealous of my brother, because I bragged about him so much. I tried to be more sensitive after that and guarded my words.

The big anniversary celebration came and went and with it, seemingly, so did our friendship. He completely gave me the cold shoulder. Tuesday mornings didn't "work" anymore. I wondered what I had done to deserve such a brush off. And then, five weeks after being diagnosed with lung cancer, my uncle, who had attended our church and was always such an encouragement, was gone. My dad's youngest brother, who seemed so healthy and alive and had laughing eyes and the deep voice that was so familiar … just gone. The grief my dad felt was palpable.

On the heels of that funeral, AP wanted the Tuesday meetings to start up again and apologized for being angry with me, saying he had felt left out. *He had felt left out?* How many times since have I asked myself how I failed to see things clearly; however, I apologized profusely for making him feel like that. For not including him in everything I did.

Now I know that he'd crossed a moral and professional boundary and had been grooming me for many months, but at the time I thought what he had told me was true—I was a spoiled brat who always got my way, and, apparently, this was my fault. I'd never even heard of clergy sexual misconduct and had no way of knowing what was really going on.

During this time, our church added an evening edition of our women's ministry meetings, which fell into my "portfolio." Each of the staff had been asked to come alongside another ministry besides our own to help and encourage. Women's ministry was mine. We had renamed the ministry Women of Worth, and we were now adding another component, which would be known as "WOWEE" —Women of Worth Evening Edition. Exciting things were happening in our women's ministry. But I was beginning to feel overloaded.

For Further Reading:

Diana Garland has written, "The reality of clergy sexual abuse of adults, usually women, is breaking on congregations and church denominations. It is a more difficult issue to understand than the abuse of children because there is the assumption that if both are adults and there is no physical coercion, then the relationship is consensual. In fact, however, when persons with power—social workers, counselors, pastors, seminary professors and administrators, pastoral and clinical supervisors, and religious employers—attempt to seduce into sexual relationships those over whom they have power, the relationship is not consensual. More than other professional roles, the ministry is liable to the blurring of roles because friendships do develop in a faith community, and the boundaries between professional and social time are often unclear" (Fortune, 1989). 8

CHAPTER FOUR
Soul Stealing

"Even a woman with a firm sense of boundaries in other kinds of relationships may well stop guarding them so that her core may be seen and known by this man." 9

IT WAS BECOMING QUITE OBVIOUS TO ME THAT I WASN'T good enough for my job and I needed AP 's opinion and suggestions to keep it. Often AP would tell me things about other people in the church, such as how duplicitous they were and how they had wronged him. I became skeptical of whom I could trust. I began to realize that I'd always been much too trusting and had been guilty of looking at the world through rose-coloured glasses. As I spent time with him, I learned not to be so open and to be more skeptical. I was also beginning to view more of life through his reality.

In the middle of everything that was going on, I began feeling like a hamster on a wheel. No matter how many hours I put in, I felt like I wasn't doing enough. Our Tuesday morning meetings sometimes stretched to an hour and half, as we would go over details that I felt I needed his input on before I moved ahead. I basically started to feel like I couldn't do my job without his approval. I had learned my lesson about not including him and wasn't going to do that again.

That fall I was once again planning for a city-wide mass choir. This would be the third time that many churches came together for a weekend concert that we called "IMAGINE." I was excited to lead the choir, because it was a great picture of the body of Christ coming together in unity. The first year we had 150 voices; the second year we again sang to a sell out crowd in our Cultural Centre.

By the third year, however, it seemed like all the steam had gone out of the program, and no one was stepping forward to help. Before my parents left on a trip, my dad encouraged me to cancel that year rather than try to do it alone. But when I told AP, he refused to consider that idea, saying he was sure that he and I could pull it off. Repeatedly, AP had undermined my dad, pointing out his weaknesses and inadequacies. Of course, everything was said "in confidence," and by now AP's influence had trumped my dad's. But I was not aware of that back then.

I found myself spending hours recording rehearsal tracks for each part and then burning 120 CDs. I scheduled four rehearsals and scrambled to find people to fill the many positions that were required.

One morning after I dropped the kids off at their different schools, I heard a strange voice for the first time. I was in the van, about three blocks away from the church, when I heard, "You are all alone. Everyone has abandoned you." I wept. I pulled the van to the side of the road and hung my head and wept. I *felt* like I was all alone. I was exhausted. I felt like the world was crashing down on me and the weight was squeezing every living breath out of my lungs. But I dried my eyes, drove to church, and told no one. That's how October and November went— hearing the voices, feeling such despair, and acting like everything was fine.

The concert came and it was bigger and better than ever. We had added a children's choir and they were amazing! We also added some media, which was very touching. All in all, it was a success, but I was glad for it to be over! I'd been finding ushers up to the last minute! That was the last Sunday in November, so our next Tuesday meeting was scheduled for December 3.

At the end of that meeting, AP leaned over his chair as though he was going to say something.

"No, I can't tell you," he said.

I told him that he could trust me, because I was a "safe person." I asked him what he was talking about, and he said that if we weren't married, this would be the time when he would ask me out. He also asked me if I would marry him if anything ever happened to our spouses.

I felt sucker punched. I've actually never been punched, but my stomach dropped, and I'm pretty sure a sucker punch would have been preferable to the hell I was about to walk into.

What did I do? That was my first thought. He was a pastor and had been a pastor for twenty-five years, so it must have been something that I had done during my three years at this church. He then said that he'd been in love with me almost from the time I'd arrived at the church.

The heart is deceitful above all else, I thought, *so he thinks he's in love with me, but I know he's not.* Not for one moment did I think of telling anyone what he had said. That would have spelled trouble for him. He trusted me with his feelings, so I couldn't betray that trust when there had been so many people in his life who had already betrayed him. I was his friend; it was my job to help him see that these feelings were just a wisp of air that may be bothering him now, but soon would be gone. I didn't know what to say, so I laughed awkwardly and jokingly said that I'd marry him and we could spend our inheritances sipping Mai Tai's on the beach. I now understand, much later, that I had already bought into the lie that I was responsible for AP's emotional wellbeing. He'd given me that responsibility by sharing painful, intimate details of his life—and I'd accepted it. I had no idea that I was opening the door to a demonic stronghold.

I stayed in for lunch that day. Sooner than I would have liked, he was back from lunch. I was sitting at my desk when he came into my office, shut the door, and stood in front of it. He seemed to fill up the space as he looked down at me.

"I don't know if this is a guy thing or not," he said, "but are you just interested in the money?"

I denied this, of course. (At that point I had no idea how much money he had.) I tried to reassure him that I cared for him, because I did. At that point, I thought of him as a close friend and my mentor. I knew I had to make him feel like I would never betray him or what he had told me in confidence.

I went home after work, got into the shower, and sobbed. How I could have been so naïve to not realize what was happening? I was filled with confusion and guilt. I had a great husband and three wonderful children, and now I didn't know what to do. My mind seemed to be filling with darkness.

I was in tears a lot that week. I knew that something was desperately wrong, but at that point couldn't put my finger on it. I remember crying like something was broken inside. Looking back, I can't believe I was so stupid and didn't realize that he had crossed a huge line.

I googled "emotional affairs," thinking I must have unwittingly initiated one, and then I called my best friend in Manitoba and asked her to pray for me, even though AP had established a confidentiality rule. I thought it would be safe, since she was two provinces away. I told her I was afraid something might happen and needed to put safeguards in place.

My friend and I had met in grade four. We started our legendary friendship by hollering across the schoolyard at each other. We just yelled "hello" and eventually started hanging out. We couldn't be more opposite. I say this with so much love: she is the most stubborn Mennonite I have ever met! And I would be dead had I never met her. She is strong and courageous and an amazing mom to an amazing young woman. She loves to laugh and can pinch you so hard you cry! I disclosed to her what had transpired between AP and myself. I begged her to pray that Satan's plans would be destroyed, and that AP would realize these feelings were completely false. Thank God, she kept that email and the ones that followed, along with the texts I sent in desperation.

Email: Dec 03, 20--

I feel the need to put a safeguard in place, and you are it. It's such a delicate topic that you're the only one I can confide in. One of the guys I work with and I are very good friends. In fact, he's confided in me things that he's only ever told his wife. It's a healthy friendship, but because we're of the opposite sex, I just feel strongly the need to pray against the plans that Satan has for us. I've never been in this situation before, and because we're right across the hall from each other ... I don't know ... I'm determined to keep this holy, but I'm only a human and need God's power to keep this pure. I'm being honest with you in that we (he and I) have even discussed this, and I know you came to mind for a reason. There's absolutely nothing amiss right now, but I'm not unaware of the devil's schemes. I just know that you will know exactly how to pray. Honestly, our friendship means so much to me. I feel like ... well, I can't believe I'm even asking you to pray about this. I told him that we need to be aware and make sure that our friendship remains pure. Do you think that we've crossed the line by talking about this?

The next day, AP seemed nervous. He asked how I was, and I said I had emailed my friend. He looked stricken, but said that he deserved that. I wasn't sure what he meant. Then we started talking about how the situation would just fizzle out. How we would each focus on our own marriages and forget he'd ever said anything. At this point, I didn't have any romantic feelings for him. My world was starting to tilt. I couldn't get his words out of my head. Never before in my life had anyone said anything like that to me, let alone someone who was successful, powerful, happily married, and so much older than I! That week was a blur. I cried so much and pleaded with God to take it all away.

The second week of December came and he was still being very nice to me. I couldn't understand it. He was attentive and encouraging and helped in every possible way he could. It was like something had flipped in him, and I now belonged to him. Somehow in my confusion I couldn't understand the change, because I'd learned the hard way to steel myself against his rapid mood changes. I remembered that only a few months earlier he'd been so rude to me after the Sunday morning service that I fell apart, and my husband had to ask my parents to take the kids to lunch so he could whisk me away. Now my head was spinning with this new act.

By week three, I felt like I was actually beginning to fall for him. Our Tuesday meetings now included discussions about our feelings for each other. He suggested we walk just close enough to the edge of right and wrong to enjoy ourselves but not fall over. He told me that he'd had feelings for me for a long time. He even remembered the shirt I'd been wearing over a year ago at a staff retreat. He showed me a file folder with what seemed like hundreds of pictures of me in it. I was stunned. I can't remember what I felt beyond blank shock. By this time, he was telling me that he loved me.

I now realize that an ungodly soul tie was beginning to form between us, or perhaps had already begun. Things began to get more physical. He would try to calm me when I became anxious about our "new relationship." I began relying on him to take care of my emotions. I believed that I really did have feelings for him, but I told him we needed to be careful because I didn't want to lose my job. He became defensive and said that even though we had a higher responsibility, he still had feelings like a normal human being.

One day we went to get some staging from the basement, and AP came up from behind me and put his hands on my shoulders. It terrified me, but by this time I was earning an academy award for faking my feelings. On the way up the stairs, I got the feeling that he was about to kiss me, so I made sure I was out of reach. Suddenly, there was a wall between us. I felt like I'd done something wrong. He briskly walked away from me, and my stomach dropped. I was confused and devastated! I couldn't stay there, so I went to my office, which was still not private enough. I then headed to the car. I intended to drive away, but it was a cold day and the car was covered in frost, so I sat there and wept.

My thoughts were so jumbled. *What had I done now to upset him?* He'd been so pleasant to me recently. Other people were also noticing the change in his mood, and I knew that it was because of me. I was trying desperately to keep him happy and confident of my care for him. He came out to the car after texting me and apologized. He admitted to being frustrated that our feelings couldn't go anywhere.

In the days to come, I had something else to worry about. During one of our meetings, he said that if I ever told anyone what was going on between us, he would refute my claims with a list of things he could use against me. I thought he was looking at a document on his computer as he talked. I felt like I was having a panic attack, but I managed an awkward laugh and asked, "Like what"? He mentioned the time he caressed the back of my head as he was hugging me after my grandma died. He now said that he would claim he was offering comfort and couldn't help it if I took it the wrong way. I can't remember what else he had prepared, but I knew that from now on, denial was the name of the game. I was absolutely devastated. It was a long time before I remembered this exchange and realized that the weird feeling I'd had when he hugged me after my grandma's death was actually because AP already was getting a sexual thrill out of touching me. I wanted to throw up when I realized that.

By this point I felt very attached to him, like I could hardly plan a song set without his approval, or move forward in anything unless he hit the GO button. We talked about how, if this relationship got out of control, there would be so many ripple effects. I thought of the sorrow it would bring the ones who love me. I think this is when I began to think, *It would be better for everyone if something terrible happened to me.* I just wished I could die.

As we set up for Christmas Eve, he talked about his assets, and claimed that if he divorced his wife, he and I could run away together. He said he wouldn't care if his children never spoke to him again; they were all adults and could figure it out for themselves. As I think back on these conversations now, I really believe he was lying about it all.

How could I have gone so quickly from feeling nothing but friendship for him to thinking he was my soul mate? My Oscar performance now extended to everyone: my parents, the staff, my friends, and, sadly, my dear husband.

One day I decided to tell another woman in our church about the situation. As we began talking, she started telling me about the depression she was battling. In caring for her, my intentions got derailed.

Around Christmas, I thought that I must be in love with AP. I didn't know which way was up or which way was down. We talked about how we were living in an alternate reality—now I realize it was his reality.

Texting became frequent. There were still things I did to upset him, though. He said later that jealousy would drive him mad, and he was frustrated that I wasn't with him all of the time.

In one of our conversations, I asked him to protect me. We both talked about how this would probably fizzle out and our lives wouldn't be affected by it. I wanted him to protect me from this relationship getting out of hand, so I asked him to protect me and trusted that he would.

He and his wife were leaving for a vacation in January, but he told me that he was creating letters and notes and things for me to open every day while he was gone. I said that was a bad idea, and that instead we should spend the time falling back in love with our spouses. I could tell that upset him, so once again I backtracked and tried my best to appease his disappointment. Much later, I learned that all the time AP was on vacation, he was also texting almost daily with another woman he had tried to groom.

On New Year's Day, he kissed me for the first time. From that point, the physical boundaries disappeared. He was again very complimentary about the way I looked. He left for Hawaii the next day and I cried. I didn't see how I was going to get through seventeen days without my "anchor."

I don't understand how he became so important to me in such a short amount of time. Until December 2, I wasn't even aware that our relationship was inappropriate. But one short month later, I had come 180 degrees. I still don't understand. I know that I was hearing voices. One voice kept telling me that I was walking the path of destruction. I would just agree with it out loud. I knew continuing this would destroy me. I sensed that AP wanted to destroy himself, and I was okay with being a part of the carnage. I don't know why. I don't know why I wanted to destroy myself— I just know that I could hardly go an hour without texting him. He called me a few times from Hawaii, and once went on the camera that's set up on the beach to talk to me. Seeing him made me miss him all the more. At this time, I began waking up consistently during the night and not sleeping well. There seemed to be darkness closing in on me.

For Further Reading:

"When your pastor began to abuse you, he used sexual language and touching to intensify your natural feelings of attachment to him. You may feel confused by the powerful effect his words and touching had on you. Victims often describe the effect of their abuser's pursuit by saying, 'It was like I'd been drugged.' In a sense you were. Recent research has shown how attachment prompted by sexual interchange triggers extraordinary levels of a hormone called Oxytocin. Once excessive amounts of Oxytocin are produced a person experiences a variety of effects. First, Oxytocin triggers a firm bond or allegiance to the person whose words and touching prompt the production of the hormone. This explains why persons who engage in a one-night stand find later that they continue to feel an attachment to the person they had sex with. Second, Oxytocin suppresses one's ordinary sense of wariness or danger. The hormone makes us set aside precautions we would ordinarily take. Finally, Oxytocin creates a sense of euphoria similar to that described by those who snort coke. The effects of Oxytocin serve well in binding us to a mate. Once we have acquired a mate, most of us do not find ourselves in relationship where the hormone is reactivated to the degree described here. Using the access he had to you as your pastor, your abuser induced a heightened sense of attachment and behavior characteristic of a person madly in love or who had been drugged. Your abuser is like the person who drops Ecstasy into his date's drink at a party and then takes advantage of her. Like people who have been drugged, victims of sexual abuse are not to be blamed." 10

CHAPTER FIVE
Shame and Trauma

"Sometimes I want to scream, 'Yes, I am a victim of clergy sexual abuse!' Yes it did happen to me. I hate the secret. I hate the burden. Why can't I talk about this the way one would talk about any other injustice? But I can't, probably because I fear there will always be someone who thinks I asked for it or wanted it." - Mikki

I CAN'T REMEMBER HOW MANY TEXTS WENT BACK AND forth that month. He also started emailing a daily poem to me, which I was supposed to immediately delete. He had all the staff passwords, so I now wonder if he ever wrote emails to himself, posing as me, to "prove his innocence" in all of this.

My body began responding to him, which added to my confusion. It was as if I was no longer myself, but had been replaced with emptiness. One day, he put his hands on my arms and shook me a little, saying how badly he needed me and asking if I'd go with him to his house. My stomach sank (I realize that happened a lot) and I hesitated, but then agreed. He said that he believed God had brought me to FSJ not just for the church, but for him as well.

The voice reminding me that I was on the path to destruction was very familiar at this point, and I started sinking further into darkness. In January, I made an appointment with a doctor to get on some antidepressants. I almost fell apart on the phone when the receptionist told me it would be a month before I could see him. I didn't think I would last another month.

By now I had to be near AP or talking to him all the time. It's as if he held all the batteries, and I wandered aimlessly without them. As far as church work went, I wouldn't make decisions about anything without first talking them through with him. I had become totally inept at my job. Our meetings became very frequent. AP told my dad that he needed to meet with me so often because I was having a tough time setting goals and objectives, and he was helping me "gain focus" in my ministry.

He once told me that as soon as this started to affect my marriage, we would be over. He was sobbing as he said this. Inside I was screaming, "Of course, you freak, it's affecting my marriage! It's killing me!" But truth wasn't part of this relationship. My job was to please, so I assured him everything was good.

After I got back from a trip, I decided to end the relationship. After our Tuesday morning greeting, I finally got the courage to say, "We have to be done. This cannot continue." I was on antidepressants by that time, but every moment of that Tuesday afternoon and evening was filled with me praying for Jesus to take me home. I believed He was going to rescue me by taking me away from this hell. Around midnight when I realized I was still alive, I was in so much distress that I emailed him and said I had changed my mind.

I had never experienced such darkness. I felt as though I'd spent the last three months walking away from Jesus, so I knew He was far away and angry with me … or maybe just sad. After I broke it off, I was suddenly in the darkness alone and could hardly breathe. At least with AP I hadn't been alone. The darkness was deep and heavy and crippling and was killing me, but I wasn't alone. The only conclusion I could come to was to keep everybody happy, even if it meant I would die inside. I earnestly began praying that Jesus would take me home.

The next day I was a basket case. I knew for certain that death was my only way out. AP came into my office and pretended to look over paperwork as we talked. I told him that I wanted to die. I shared with him some of the plans I was thinking about, like driving over a cliff. He looked stricken. I wanted to die so badly.

He tried to comfort me, but it left me feeling no different than before—except that now I wasn't in the pit of hell alone anymore, because AP was with me. I began researching how to overdose—not a pretty picture. I read that overdosing on over-the-counter drugs could leave you in a life of physical misery and agony. You wouldn't die, but you'd likely spend the rest of your life wishing you had. The other option was letting the car run in the garage, but every time I thought about that, I thought of one my children finding me and what that would do to them.

I decided to keep everybody happy until I could die. I phoned my friend again: "I just need you to pray with me that God will take me home." I knew that I couldn't stay in this life and keep everyone happy, so I hoped that God would literally strike me down and hopefully not send me to hell. I knew my family would be okay. In fact, they would likely be better off.

I knew my friend in Manitoba was concerned. What I didn't know was that although I had sworn her to secrecy, she was so concerned about my suicidal thoughts that she shared them with her pastor's wife, who immediately counselled her to phone my parents. So on a Wednesday afternoon in March, my parents got the news that I was in an inappropriate relationship with AP and that my friend was afraid for my life.

Because the associate pastor was involved, my parents felt they needed to contact the District Office. They did so, and were told that this situation needed to be "contained" and that the District Office would handle everything.

Five days later, I was in my office when one of the men from the District Office walked in and asked if he could talk to me. Instantly I knew what this was about, and I felt my stomach twist and grab every internal organ in my body. I immediately texted AP and told him who was in my office. This man is a very big man and seemed to fill my office until there was no more air. I couldn't breathe.

He sat down and said there were allegations of an inappropriate relationship between me and AP. I played dumb. The only thing I could think of was to deny it, because AP had told me that if I ever came out with allegations against him, he had a list of statements to refute anything I said. I told him that we'd hugged and kissed a few times.

I madly texted AP and told him what I'd said. He asked how many times I'd confessed to. I said five. He didn't like that. Then he had to go. The man from the District Office was a huge, intimidating giant, and all I could think of was how he and AP had been friends for many years. They'd known each other for a lifetime. They had attended college together, and were both big players. I wanted to get away from him.

I found my parents waiting in my dad's office. There were many tears and hugs, and I was shaking violently. The man asked me not to text AP about any of this. I lied to him about the extent of what had happened, and then I lied when I agreed not to text AP .

My mom drove me home, because I was still shaking too hard to drive. My husband was home sick, so we were going to go tell him what had transpired. Later that day, my dad was instructed to take away my keys and phone. I found out that it was nearly two weeks later that AP's keys were taken away. That fact figured prominently in the days to come.

The last contact I had with AP was via Facebook, when I told him that my phone had been taken away. I felt like I'd been axed in half. The pain was excruciating. I've never felt so dark and so alone. On Monday night, my mom and I were sitting downstairs. I looked at her, longing to tell her the whole truth. Finally, I disclosed everything to her. She prayed over me and then we went to the District Office representative, and I disclosed everything again. I felt like I was absolutely betraying AP , but at this point I made the decision to put my husband first. After my conversation with the representative, I returned home and told my husband the rest.

Thursday night the demons began screaming at me … literally. Flashbacks of conversations and pictures of what we had done were thrown into my face. It was like grotesque beings screaming past me in warp speed as I sat there in terror. I have a tangible memory of demonic forces snarling and reaching for me. For about four hours, I sat on the couch, trying to calm down. Morning came and a dear friend (who didn't know any details except that I was going through a hard time) let me know that she had spent hours praying for me in the middle of the night. I was astonished that Jesus would wake her up and cause her to pray for me while I was battling the darkest fight I've ever been engaged in. I felt so unworthy.

The next day, my mom and a friend and I read through information on soul ties. I knew that I couldn't go on like I was. I needed to be free, and I desperately hoped this would help. My mom explained that the Bible speaks of soul ties when it talks about souls being knit together, or becoming one flesh. A soul tie can serve different functions, but in it's simplest form, it ties two souls together in the spiritual realm. Godly soul ties can draw a married couple together and knit their hearts to each other. Ungodly soul ties can cause a beaten and abused woman attach to a man from whom, in the natural realm, she would run.

In the demonic world, unholy soul ties serve as a bridge between two people through which evil can pass. A soul tie may allow a person to manipulate and control another without that person being aware. As I listened, I realized that what I thought was "love" was nothing more than an ungodly soul tie through which a demon of lust had free reign. I prayed through that prayer, asking God to forgive and cancel any ground or permission I had given over to Satan. I declared that the demons had no right in my life and commanded them to leave. I claimed the victory that Jesus' death had won on Calvary, and *immediately* felt freedom! I no longer felt the desire to text AP. In fact, I wanted to get rid of all the pictures and souvenirs he had given me. I went to my office to get them and found that *they were all gone*. I knew that AP was the only person who knew where I'd hidden them, and I knew he still had his church keys. I felt so betrayed. I felt lied to. I felt like he hated me and was throwing me to the wolves. BUT I WAS FREE! I WAS FREE! I felt nothing for him. I immediately recognized that what I'd thought was love was all a lie.

My denomination has a disciplinary protocol, and because they were firmly convinced that my situation was a consensual affair, I was questioned and examined by three committees comprised of people within the denomination. I felt humiliated and confused every time I had to repeat my story.

In the beginning, I didn't have a clear understanding of clergy sexual abuse or what had happened to me, and I believe I incriminated myself more than once by accepting all the blame. Consequently, I was given a two-year probation.

Interestingly, in the days and weeks and months following, other women began to come forward with complaints against AP , and a small group of people tried to convince the denominational leadership, as well as our church elders, that my case needed to be re-evaluated. A good friend of ours who has dealt with sexual abuse for many years put together a paper detailing clergy sexual abuse and soul ties. Although he offered to meet with the church elders, they (with two exceptions) refused to even listen to his presentation. They would not consider it as anything but a "consensual affair." As far as we know, the leadership didn't consult with anyone outside of their denomination.

My father's employment as senior pastor was terminated six months later, because he wouldn't agree with their conclusion, and because he kept lobbying for the other women who had also been victimized. I let the denomination know that I did not want to be reinstated after the two-year period, and we have all moved away from that community.

For Further Reading:

"Every clergy or minister is a symbol of religious authority. By virtue of the pastoral office, the minister interprets religious truth, the meaning of life, the way of faith, and even the reality of God (Chibnall, Wolf, & Duckro, 1998; Poling, 2005; Robinson, 2004). Add to that status the power of the pastor's presence through ministry, and the special influence a minister holds among his or her congregation. In addition, female clergy supervised by senior male clergy may develop a special trust that can lead to openness and vulnerability. Feeling bonds of trust and affirmation, female clergy may bring the vulnerable, wounded, and intimate sides of themselves into the relationship, seeking acceptance, emotional support, and a role model. When the male clergy exploits his privileged position for personal sexual satisfaction he violates a sacred trust that is contrary to Christian morals, doctrine, and canon laws.

"Because of the respect and even reverence the position carries, there is an imbalance of power and hence a vulnerability inherent in the ministerial relationship (Chibnall, Wolf, & Duckro, 1998; Poling, 2005; Robinson, 2004). In these circumstances, this imbalance of power makes it the responsibility of the church leader to maintain appropriate emotional and sexual boundaries with colleagues. Once violated, the female clergy may feel deep shame or self-condemnation. She may be afraid others will not believe her or fear being blamed by church officials or members. The sad consequence is that many times the female clergy can experience a crisis of faith and even leave the Church altogether, believing that neither God nor the body of Christ was present in her suffering (Francis & Turner, 1995). Sexual harassment may affect prayer, one's image of God, and one's relationship to God (Chibnall, Wolf, & Duckro, 1998)." 12

CHAPTER SIX
The Healing Power of Grief

"The brain can produce emotional responses in us that have very little to do with what we think we're dealing with or talking about or thinking about at the time. In other words, emotional reactions can be elicited independent of our conscious thought processes. For example, we've found pathways that take information into the amygdala without first going through the neocortex, which is where you need to process it in order to figure out exactly what it is and be conscious of it. So, emotions can be and, in fact, probably are mostly processed at an unconscious level. We become conscious and aware of all this after the fact.

"...journaling after emotional experiences allows us to process them when we can understand them cognitively and (in some cases) *consciously* for the first time." 13

It was almost two years before I was able to journal again. During that time, my husband and I were in counselling with someone we have come to love and deeply respect. One of the important things I learned was that I needed to see my memories as triggers that had the ability of creating a foothold for demons to harass me. I learned to pray against strongholds and break through the lies of Satan that were giving me panic attacks. My husband was able to process his own devastation and grief. He battled through his own pain, and with our friend's help he even learned how to pray warfare prayers for our marriage and for me.

One of the lies I had to work against was the belief that I should have been able to stop this. In other words, deep inside I still believed I'd caused the whole thing. But I found freedom as I gained understanding of how the brain works to take over in times of stress and reverts to the way I would typically respond to stress. I learned that my way of coping was to blame myself and then freeze, becoming unable to make healthy choices.

Journaling helped me sort things out, giving me a tool to make some sense of my thoughts and fears and grief.

December 6

Today has been a DAY. Can't seem to get the grief or sadness or bewilderment out of my mind. Two years ago, I was hearing voices telling me I was all alone. Two years ago, I was desperately trying to figure out how to put up a wall between me and AP without hurting his feelings or without him knowing. Two years ago, I never would have imagined the tormented truth of what had transpired, what was happening, and what the future would hold. I was busy, busy, busy getting Christmas programs organized for the worship arts and women's ministry departments. I was excited about the Christmas Eve service. I had just come out of a successful "IMAGINE" concert. I was almost having an out of body experience. At least that what it seems like when I think back to that time. I was consumed with keeping everyone happy and unoffended.

I remember the feeling of my stomach dropping when he got me alone in the basement. When he put his hands on my shoulders I wanted to run, but felt cemented into place. Going up the stairs he almost kissed me. I almost threw up. Then he gave me the cold shoulder, so I fell apart.

When I think about that time, I wonder about verses that say God's presence is always with us. That He leads us into the green pastures and valleys. Did He turn away His gaze? He has set us beside him in the heavenly realms, but do we get removed? When could

I have walked away? Why, why, why? What happened to the power of the Holy Spirit inside of me?

So now the residual grief. It's not debilitating like it was. The friendships are gone. The ministry is gone. The church family is gone.

But I can't end an entry without being grateful for what God has done. Come and see what God has done! I am married to a man who loves me fiercely and has fought for me in the spiritual realm. I have three children who are precious gifts. And I'm singing again.

December 8

When our second child was born, my blood pressure dipped so low that I began to feel as though I was floating and seeing myself and the room from a higher vantage point. When I think back to the trauma, that's how I feel. Inside I was terrified and confused, but my shell could only just agree and oblige every request. When he gripped my arms and was shaking with how badly he said he needed to be with me, again my stomach dropped, and I knew somehow that I was getting carried further into darkness. The confusion came from how my physical body absolutely betrayed me. It not only waved a white flag of surrender, but propelled me into his arms. When I look back on all of this, I see myself responding almost robotically, but outwardly I looked like a woman in love. I resigned myself to keeping my husband happy and AP happy with the hopes that soon it would all be over and I would be dead. I would play out how my mom would help everyone through my death. How my children would get through it. How much better off (my husband) would be, anyway. I imagined them moving to his parents' home and wondered what their lives would look like. I wrote out letters to all of them in my mind. Goodbye letters.

From December 2 to 24 something ... in fact many things ... happened, because I went from feeling nothing but friendship for him to thinking he was my soul mate. It's hysterical now. When I compare him to (my husband), there's really no comparison. One is a man, and one is a cowardly predator.

I clearly remember wanting to tell a friend, but she started telling me about the depression she was battling against. Another friend I might have told was herself suicidal.

My husband's love has been Jesus' love. He has been Jesus with skin on to me.

December 16

Listening to Kari Jobe on my Christmas playlist and remembering that last Christmas Eve service. There was a dancer on stage. She was in white and was breathtaking, dancing against a background of softly falling snow. I remember feeling so much sadness, because I would have to say goodbye to AP . We were leaving for Christmas, and I wasn't sure if I'd see him before they left for Hawaii. That Christmas was marked by so many texts. I feel like I was totally absent from my family, and that makes me angry. He took a whole Christmas from my kids and from (my husband). I feel dirty and stupid when I think about that. Pathetic. He gave me a kiss on the cheek after the Christmas Eve services. They had been a giant success, complete with a string quartet playing in the lobby where everyone was invited to help themselves to our hot chocolate bar. I didn't know that he would tell me he wanted to have sex with me the next time I saw him. I really believed all of this would be over soon and before anything physical happened.

I came back from Christmas and he kissed me. My memory of it grosses me out. I can't think of fancier words than that. I feel almost physically a little sick when I think about it. Months later, I would dream that he's kissing me, and all of a sudden, his face would melt into my hands, like he'd turned into putty and was coming apart in my hands. I would wake up absolutely terrified.

This week, I've fought the sadness. Last night choir was amazing. Someone told me I was born to sing! I think you likely always sound good when you have a choir and orchestra accompanying you. Today was a good day because (my husband) was home. He's working tonight, so after supper I'm going out with the kids to buy a Rudolph headband for my youngest.

December 24

I can't help but keep thinking "two years ago …" I'm wondering who's all involved in the services. Part of me wants to weep, but that's a tiring thought. I'll just wait on that for a while! There's something so sacred in our memories. Ever since I was small, I remember being involved in the Christmas Eve services. Afterwards, we would come home and open our stockings and just be together. Often, we'd get into the car and start driving to Grandma's house. White snow as far as the eye could see!

January 1

Two years ago he leaned over to me and said, "I really want to make love to you." I immediately felt sick, and I think tears came to my eyes as I asked him to protect me. To never let anything like that ever, ever happen, because I'd lose my job and so many people would be hurt. I trusted him. I thought he had my best interest in mind. The f…ing bastard. That's all. I want to double over for the pain it causes right now. It's like my insides are recoiling at the memory. Why couldn't I have stopped it? If I could turn myself inside out, maybe I could scrape all the memories away. I don't want this memory. I don't want this story today. Tomorrow maybe I'll feel like waving the flag of God's victory, but today I want to pity myself and hide… maybe cry, eat, and watch Netflix until bed.

My parents left today. We're going out to the farm to shoot guns (which actually may be therapeutic) and have fondue for dinner.

I keep having dreams. Every night for the past five or so. About leading worship in (the church) now or about different people or dead people—zombies. You know, nice things like that. The night of the zombie dream I actually woke up. After (my husband) prayed for me, I slept well.

Today is a good day for the rapture. I may get stuck in a broom closet, though, if it happened. No ... of course I know that if Jesus walked through my door right now, He would crush me against Himself and say how much He really loved me. It just seems like it's going to take a monumental effort to be social.

January 3

I'm so glad I made it through December! Every time Chris Tomlin's "Emmanuel, Hallowed Manger Ground" came on, I would think about how AP always played games with my mind. He'd be so encouraging, and then we'd sing this song and he'd make sure I knew he disapproved. I made myself listen and enjoy it this year, and last night after I led worship, I didn't feel like doubling over in pain and weeping. Every time I've sung since I've been rescued, that's what happens. It took a lot to get back up with the choir after my solo, but last night, there was peace and JOY! This was so interesting, because the day before was such a hard day for me. I just don't want to live in fear of anything.

January 6

Woke up feeling the familiar elephant of grief sitting on my chest. I dreamt last night that I was back at (the church) and was able to embrace those people and pity them. But then I walked past AP and turned back and looked him in the face and said how much I despised him. Then I slapped him across the face. This morning I'm just feeling the betrayal I guess. I could sit and cry a while if I didn't need to get lunches and breakfast made. I'm listening to worship music, because I know it will affect and minister to me deep in my heart. When I focus on Jesus, the power of the sadness disperses, because He has been good to me. His mercies are fresh every single day. And I'm so grateful.

January 9

So the question of whether or not to brave another church service … yes, that is the question. I'm frustrated today. I feel like our kids don't have friends here. Another price to be paid, and that makes me angry. Not like there were so many friends there for our son, but the girls had quite the social calendar, and at least he had youth to go to.

I watched a movie yesterday in which the main character had the ability to go back to any moment in his life and relive it. Oh, how I wish I could do that. I've replayed his proposal a million times in my mind. My favourite outcome is standing up and slapping him across the face as hard as I possibly can. Then I go into my office and call my parents. At the same time, I let the staff know what had just happened. But once the scenario plays out in my mind, I am left again with reality. And today that makes me weep.

I guess the only way to have protected myself would have been to stand up for myself from the very beginning. When he would be a jerk to me, I should have called him on it instead of ignoring it and trying my best to respect my elder, the one in authority above me. One of the elders said there was no power imbalance. Who was at every elder's meeting? Who was in charge when my dad was gone? Who signed checks and set up accounts and passwords and a million other little details?

I just don't know what to do with all of those people. I pity them and at the same time want to erase them from my memory. If only we had stayed in Indiana. If only, if only, if only, if only!

I did my best. I shared my heart. I was vulnerable. I was so honoured to be in that position. It was like I had been created for the purpose of leading others in worship. And there were so many moments when the presence of God was palpable. So many more that could have happened. There were friendships and relationships I thought I could trust.

People will say all kinds of things, won't they? Like pledging allegiance to the man who stands almost alone for the truth. But what happened? How did everyone turn on my dad?

I surprised myself yesterday by tearing up when I thought about how much I missed my job.

So, back to church. I sit there so critical and judgemental and argue with God about why He's not helping me have a good attitude. And then a familiar song will be played, and I'll connect to the music, to the lyrics, and to the presence of Jesus.

Today is just a low day. I've been so exhausted the past couple of days … fell asleep before 9:30 last night.

January 11

Grief catches you in surprising places sometimes. Like today, I was sitting at the endocrinologist's office and I told her that two years ago I went through a significant trauma, which may have thrown my thyroid out of whack. She asked what kind of trauma. I caught my breath as tears came to my eyes and my heart started racing. She immediately apologized and asked if anything happened to my neck, which struck me as funny. I wish! Five minutes later as she was checking my pulse, my heartbeat was still high and she apologized again.

But I still maintain my streak of no panic attacks. Somebody give me a chip!

I was hearing about the happenings at (the church). Another victim was asked to go see AP, because he's "changed". I wonder why they haven't reached out to us to reconcile. Yes, the interim pastor has been teaching them on forgiveness, so I guess they're all ready to forgive and forget. Wow. What exactly are they forgiving? Even if they believed it was an affair, isn't it weird that AP would be pursuing another woman at the same time that he was after me? I'm not very schooled in the art of affairs, but something doesn't seem to make sense with that.

I've come so very far. I didn't even shed a tear about the church or the people. I just pity them. What would God be able to do if He was welcomed in spirit and in truth? I would venture to say that nobody who still attends (the church) really knows what went on—not only the grooming and abuse, but the after-waves of abuse that came at the hands of the denomination and then the elders themselves. I know I'll likely never see most of those people, if any, ever again in my life. That brings a lot of peace.

January 20

I was looking on YouTube for the videos AP made of the CD recording night. I couldn't find them, but I did find something that was posted last year … (a musician) and someone else on stage; I couldn't see the drummer. Feels sad to see them. I thought we were friends. This week I was reminded of the meeting I had with the whole worship arts community. I was talking about how the communion table beckons everyone. The invitation is for all. Some guys started talking about how the non-believer invites damnation to his soul if he partakes of communion. They totally missed the point, and I wonder if they've missed Jesus completely. Anyway, four of the guys I thought would understand were all there, and they just sat there silently. They didn't say one word in my defense, or even in defense of the Lord's invitation. I left that meeting feeling so hurt. I thought these guys had my back. I thought they saw the vision of what this team could be. I remember telling AP about it the next day, and he said his wife had been so proud of how I stood my ground. Interesting. Did they start making plans then?

I'm listening to the CD as I type this. I feel like it's a stranger singing. Part of who I was is gone. It was stolen. Evil did that. No panic attacks today. Not since the endo asked me what trauma I had been through. I still feel sorry for her, because she felt so bad! I'm sorry things turned out the way they did. I'm sorry men were too prideful to allow Jesus to speak clearly to them. To understand truth.

Since I was going down memory lane, I went on FB and looked at old staff church pictures. AP told me once he remembered everything, so he remembered a shirt I wore on a little staff retreat. He said he had been in love with me since then. That was two years before, I think. I'm pretty sure he was also pursuing (someone else) at the same time. That shirt is in the garbage.

We spent four years developing friendships and relationships, and with the exception of maybe eight people, it's all gone. Almost everything was severed. I can't describe the agony or the ripping of flesh and bone and muscle. But for so many weeks, that's how I felt. Like part of me was just a mangled mess.

Grief is a funny thing. It plays hide and seek with your most sacred emotions and feelings. And just when you think your sad spell is over, something triggers a memory and you pull out an old CD and …

I think one day the good memories will surface and the bad ones will remain a distant memory. At least that's what I hope.

February 7

I am undone. Almost two years after I was set free, I'm weeping and grieving like the wounds are fresh. I was praying almost daily for God to take me home. But He didn't. I'm tired of the bloody mess and lies and deceit and trauma.

March 13

The song rolling around in my head has been "You're a good, good Father, that's who You are, and I'm loved by You, that's who I am". Two short years ago I was in an intense battle. When I look back now, I see that it was the beginning of freedom. The darkest hours, the spiritual warfare was all just the beginning of the healing journey that we've been on for two years now. It was this time two years ago when I woke up in the middle of the night and just couldn't sleep, so finally I got up and watched some Netflix. As I watched the shows, it was as if demons were screaming at me. The start of *Star Wars* has a bunch of writing against a backdrop of stars before going into hyper-speed. The stars shoot past you so fast, they blur together. That's how this night was. Demons were literally screaming past my mind and head for about four hours. The next morning, I was ready for some release, so my mom led me through the soul ties prayer and information. As soon as that prayer was finished, I was freed from all my feelings for him. I didn't feel the need to call or talk to him. It was amazing. I want to forget what happened between December and March. I wish I could erase everything.

***

I'm learning that processing our losses is hard and painful work. A loss uproots us. It's like pulling a plant out of the soil … tearing it away from its nourishing connection with the soil. But as we do the necessary grief work, we slowly return the plant to the life-sustaining soil, and we feel life coming back.

If we don't deal with the loss or the wound, a scab forms that's always tender to the touch, because the wound has not been cleansed. And we're paralyzed—we can't go forwards or backwards. We're stuck. Over the years, that grief morphs into bitterness and unforgiveness, and we end up miserable. It's just a lot easier to keep on with the business of simply making a good living and making sure we never rock the boat.

Sometimes we need to make a decision. First of all, we need to ADMIT that there are wounds that have never been dealt with. We can't go back to the past to relive the good times or to seek revenge for the bad times, but we need to go back to grieve—because that legitimizes our pain and helps us let go.

In other words, we need to go back to that place of pain and say, "There is a logical reason for my feeling." We need to stop saying, "I should be over it by now! I need to stop babying myself! It was my fault!" Deciding to be gentle with ourselves is the first step to dealing with the past.

Grieving a loss isn't easy. Sometimes we don't even recognize our losses. We may experience a painful event and fail to identify it as a loss. Other times we almost consciously shut the door, trying to forget rather than feel the pain again. However, ungrieved loss is one of the precursors to shame—that insidious feeling that holds us in a death-grip until we make a decision to open our hearts to what has been carefully buried for a long time.

We begin to feel ashamed because we feel that we are somehow defined by what happened. We believe that we've forever changed—our very identity has been marred. This is especially true in the case of sexual abuse. Even though the person abused was the victim, he or she is the one who carries the feeling of being dirty, used, and somehow marred.

Shame is a painful feeling about ourselves: "I don't like who I am." We see ourselves as less valuable. Someone has called it "the hemorrhage of the soul." Shame destroys our sense of wholeness and leaves us fragmented. It's different than guilt. Guilt tells me I made a mistake; shame shouts that I am a mistake. It seems like there is no possibility of repair, because shame is a matter of identity, not behaviour.

Shame occurs within relationships. It's a feeling that I am weak, foolish, or undesirable before the eyes of someone who's important to me. It's relational because it always occurs from the vantage point of another. Someone sees me for who I really am, and I am inadequate! We internalize what we believe others think about us, and we are ashamed.

It must be emphasized that most people don't even recognize shame for what it is. Instead, we develop strategies to keep away from the pain of exposure. We describe ourselves with words such as "stupid," "weak," "ugly," "ignorant," and "clumsy."

Many deep feelings come along with shame: anger, rage, fear, and more. We may shut down areas of ourselves, fearing that to be who we really are would only invite ridicule. If our innocence has been stolen for someone else's pleasure, we may shut the door on our value as sexual beings. In a sense, it's easier to feel depressed than to deal with the shame.

How can we deal with shame? First, we must legitimize our pain. One of the most helpful ways to do that is through writing. There is no right or wrong way to do this; everyone does it in their own way. Some write to the person who was harmed, others write to the abuser, and still others write to God. Writing in this way releases the emotional energy that has been held captive. In fact, recent research has shown that putting a pen to paper actually produces benefits that can be measured by brain scans.

Next, we need to spend time asking ourselves what beliefs we cling to as a result of being harmed. Which ones are true, and which ones need to be replaced with truth? After all, it is TRUTH that sets us free! If we can do this very important work in the presence of a friend who will listen and make no judgements, we are most fortunate.

It took a year for me to realize what had been done to me, and another year of therapy with our counsellor to process everything. A few more years have passed since I disclosed the abuse, and I'm amazed at the healing God has brought. My husband has become the warrior of our family. He is the most honest, courageous man of God I've ever met. By the grace of God, I'm alive today. And I'm so thankful.

My life has been privileged. I have a loving family and a healthy marriage, but I've seen and lived in the darkness. I know what oppression feels like, and I've heard demonic voices urging me to end my life. I've begged Jesus to take me to heaven, and I know the deep wounds of betrayal. But I've seen my Almighty Father take up my fight. I've seen Jesus with skin on as my husband has prayed warfare prayers over me. I've been released from strongholds and had a front row seat to watching God make an absolute spectacle of the enemy.

We stopped attending church for about eighteen months. Our counsellor even gave me permission to avoid the Bible, since it had been a part of the abuse. Over the past two years, though, my Father has wooed me back to Himself. I never thought I'd sing again, and now I can sing and lead worship without doubling over in physical pain afterwards. I'm learning to trust people with my eyes wide open. I've learned that most of us will never know the depth of each other's stories, but the cross ... at the cross ... at the foot of the cross, our stories all become The Story! It's all about Jesus. When people betray us and lie about us, it becomes obvious that we aren't fighting against flesh and blood.

There are no secrets in a healthy church. That was our mantra as we began seeking a church to call home when we moved away from the city where the abuse took place. As I walked into the church we're attending once again, the tears came as I remembered the safe place this used to be for me, and the growing up I did here. As we sat in the service as a family on our first

Sunday back, my husband leaned over and said, "This is our church."

I am a worshipper. Every time I get on stage, I thank the Lord for the joy it is to serve Him with the gifts He has given me. Being involved in different churches has given me an appreciation for unity. We all bring stuff to the table. Most of it needs to be pushed off as we listen to hear what Jesus wants to say to us as a church, and as a child of God. Worship is a lifestyle. Personal ministry time with Jesus has to be where the most powerful moments of worship happen in order for public ministry to be authentic. For me, that's sitting at the piano, singing scripture or reading the Word and journalling prayers and listening for His voice. But it's also serving my family and loving them well. Let me be clear—I have not arrived. I'm a work in progress. I love that He delights in us, in our weaknesses, and in our growing pains!

If you are seeking personal help or are interested in a deeper understanding of clergy sexual abuse, I have a good friend, Elsie Goerzen, who works at Mennonite Central Committee (MCC) in Abbotsford, BC. She coordinates the End Abuse Program. Her work includes When Love Hurts support groups for women who have experienced abuse in their intimate relationship, and Home Improvement: Men in Relationship support and accountability groups for men voluntarily participating. She can be reached at 604-845-0841 (cell) or 604-851-7725 (direct line at MCC). She also offers workshops on Understanding

Sexual Abuse by a Church Leader or Caregiver.
email: elsiegoerzen@mccbc.ca
www.http://abuseresponseandprevention.ca

CHAPTER SEVEN
A Pastoral Response

I WAS DELIGHTED WHEN OUR FRIEND AND COUNSEL-
lor, Dr. Steve Masterson, agreed to write a personal
letter for this book. As you read it, you will not only
hear his heart, but, hopefully, the heart of the Heavenly
Father, whose voice I have heard many times while
talking with Steve.

Dear Friend,

As you have read this book, you may have realized
for the very first time that you were a victim of clergy
sexual abuse, or this may be the first time you realized
that you are not alone. If that is the case, I would like
to share my heart with you.

Clergy sexual abuse is one of the darkest expressions of evil rooted in the depravity of the human heart. Jesus said in Matthew 15:19, *"For out of the heart come evil thoughts ... sexual immorality."* Jeremiah the prophet said in Jeremiah 17: 9, *"The heart is deceitful above all things and beyond cure. Who can understand it?"*

A Partnership with Evil

A person who takes on the role of pastor has been called of God to shepherd the Bride of Christ, His church. Paul writes in 1 Timothy 3:1–7 that if anyone such as an overseer (pastor/clergy) wants to provide leadership in the church he must be above reproach, self controlled, respectable, not violent but gentle, and committed to his wife. He needs to be thought well of or else the Devil will figure out a way to lure him into a trap This clearly describes the Biblical standard for a pastor or member of the clergy, and it defines what his heart should look like.

However, the minister who abused you was lured into the devil's trap, and therefore came under the demonic authority of evil. His actions towards you then became orchestrated by evil; as a result, you were wounded in your spirit and soul, and your identity as an image bearer was broken.

The Apostle Peter uses graphic language to warn us that *"Your enemy the devil prowls around like a roaring lion looking for someone to devour"* (1 Peter 5:8). Clergy sexual abuse is one of the ways evil tries to destroy both the abuser and the victim.

Unless our understanding of clergy/pastor sexual abuse includes a deeper realization of the nature of the abuser's spiritual relationship and partnership with the powers of darkness, we will not fully recognize how intense the spiritual battle is. Paul teaches us so clearly from Ephesians 6:12: *"For our struggle is not just against flesh and blood, but against the rulers, against the authorities, and against the powers of this dark world, and against the spiritual forces of evil in the heavenly realms."*

The Evil Schemes and Strategies Satan Uses in Clergy Sexual Abuse

All of the lies that your abuser used to deceive you came from the father of lies, Satan (John 8:44). The subtle relational seduction under the guise of pastoral/staff friendship, the slow manipulating power of the grooming process, the threats if secrets are broken, the literal brainwashing that profoundly impacted your mind and thought processes, ending in a loss of sound reasoning, led to a perverted, twisted distortion of spirit, soul, and body oneness between you and the one who abused you. You may remember the confusion that left you feeling like you were caught in the devil's trap with no way out. And when you were at the point of greatest vulnerability and mental confusion, your abuser was able to start crossing sexual boundaries—physically or emotionally.

Your story may be similar to my friend's, or it may be different; however as you read through her story, I hope you began to understand that while evil was using her abuser to bring harm and brokenness, God was already working to undo the destruction and bring freedom for her and glory for Himself. Freedom came as she was able to disclose what was going on, even though she was confused and struggling with Satan's lie that "she must have done something to cause it."

I can personalize Romans 8:26–27 for my friend, and I encourage you to make this truth your own: "The Holy Spirit helped my friend in her distress. For she didn't even know what she should pray for, but the Holy Spirit prayed for her with groanings that cannot be expressed in words. And the Father who knows all hearts knew what the Spirit was saying, for the Spirit was pleading for her in harmony with God's own will."

The secret to letting God always make something good out of our lives is to allow Him to define what that "good" is to look like and accomplish for his glory.

A Fight to the Finish—Ephesians 6:10-16

> God is strong, and he wants you strong. So take everything the Master has set out for you, well-made weapons of the best materials. And put them to use so you will be able to stand up to everything the Devil throws your way. This is no afternoon athletic contest that we'll walk away from and forget about in a couple of hours. This is for keeps, a life-or-death fight to the finish against the Devil and all his angels.

Be prepared. You're up against far more than you can handle on your own. Take all the help you can get, every weapon God has issued, so that when it's all over but the shouting you'll still be on your feet. (Ephesians 6:10–13, MSG)

Stand firm then, with the belt of truth buckled around your waist, with the breastplate of righteousness in place, and with your feet fitted with the readiness that comes from the gospel of peace. In addition to all this, take up the shield of faith, with which you can extinguish all the flaming arrows of the evil one. Take the helmet of salvation and the sword of the Spirit, which is the word of God. (Ephesians 6:14–17, NIV)

Put these pieces of armour on as you continue your healing journey:

Use the BELT OF TRUTH to break the power of the strongholds from all the deception that came from the father of lies.

May your heart be freshly covered with the Lord's BREAST PLATE OF RIGHTEOUSNESS, bringing healing to your soul and sexual brokenness, as well the breaking the perverted spirit, soul, and body bonds and ties with your abuser.

May your feet be FITTED WITH THE SHOES OF THE GOSPEL OF PEACE to replace all the fears that have tormented and kept you trapped.

Lift THE SHIELD OF FAITH to cover yourself from all the strategies, schemes, plans, and weapons of the enemy that he used to deceive, accuse, harass, manipulate, groom, seduce, and threaten you.

Place on your head once again the LORD'S HELMET OF SALVATION, protecting your mind from all the confusion and subtle brainwashing, as well as breaking the power of all the secrets.

Continue to take everything to God in PRAYER and use the SWORD OF THE SPIRIT, the living Word of God, to give strength and wisdom and courage.

A Final Blessing

God has been so merciful and gracious in healing my friend, Kristal, whose story you have just read. He has restored to her the joy of worshipping, loving, and serving Him with all her heart.

And I know He will do the same for you. I've personalized the following verses for you:

> The LORD will come and bind up your broken heart. He has proclaimed freedom for you from your captive and has comforted you as you have grieved what the enemy stole from you. The LORD has and will continue to bestow on you his crown of beauty and remove

the ashes of shame and evil perpetrated against you. He has anointed you with the oil of gladness to heal you from your season of grieving and mourning. He has dressed you in a garment of worship and praise instead of a spirit of despair, all for you to be his display of his glory and splendor. (Isaiah 61:1)

I the LORD will always be with you because it is I who saved you from your enemies. I will always enjoy taking great delight in you as I continually quiet you with my love and rejoice over you with singing. Know this, that every time you sing and worship me, your voice will be a true echo of me singing over you! (Zephaniah 3:17,

I will leave you with some words from 2 Corinthians 3:2–3: which I have again personalized just for you: You are God's story that he has written on your heart to be read and sung to everybody. A story written by Christ, written not with ink, but with the Spirit of the Living God, and not on tablets of stone but on the tablets of your heart.

The story that Kristal has written on these pages is not her own. It is God's story of rescue and beauty. He is the most awesome Author, Editor, Choreographer, and Publisher. God is also writing His story in and through your life, and any evil ever intended to harm you will always be used for your good and to bring Him all the glory, honour, and praise that belongs to Him.

Dr. Steve Masterson BRE, MA, MA, Doctor of Divinity

CHAPTER EIGHT
Helping Victims of Clergy Sexual Abuse

YOU MAY HAVE READ THIS BOOK BECAUSE SOMEONE you know and love is struggling with abuse by a pastor or other professional. And you're wondering how you can help them.

The most important thing you can do is to let your friend know that you believe her and what happened is not her fault. You can help her realize that disclosing takes tremendous strength and courage. She will begin to regain power that has been taken from her when she is able to see that her abuser's behaviour was wrong and needed to be stopped. But power will not be regained without hard work and strong support from you. Church leaders as well as congregations almost always blame the survivor for the fall of a religious leader, calling it an "affair". They assume because she was an adult and not violently assaulted, the relationship must have been consensual. When my story was clearly presented to the elder's board in my church, one of the elders exclaimed, "that's a textbook case of Professional Abuse. We've been trained in understanding these kinds of power differences, etc." However those who wanted to protect the minister who abused me were able to lobby successfully and silence the few who could have spoken truth.

That brings up the next point: make sure the survivor has an advocate. Denominations that have created a protocol for dealing with clergy sexual abuse will have already provided for this in their document. It's important to impress on the survivor that she should never meet with anyone involved in the investigation without someone to support her. I was required to repeat my story three times to three different groups of people. I was thankful that I was at least allowed to have someone with me during this shameful and painful retelling.

Language is critical. A disclosure always exacerbates the trauma as well as the shame and the pain. Make sure the survivor clearly understands the meaning of coercion, power differences, and grooming. At the end of one of my sessions with denominational leadership, one of the women said to me, "I'm sorry that we as a denomination didn't do a better job of protecting you." At that time her words were confusing because I still believed I was at fault and up to that point they had done nothing to help me understand anything other than that. I didn't have language to comprehend what she was actually saying.

And because I didn't know the right language to use, I fell short of naming my experience in a way that reflected the deep damage done by the predator. At the final "disciplinary" meeting, I was told that the way I had answered questions at the beginning, (in the midst of the trauma of disclosing), gave them grounds to label the relationship between AP and myself as a "consensual affair".

Ultimately, healing involves forgiving, which, I am learning, is a very long process. However often the community and the church urges survivors to forgive even before healing has begun. Diana Garland's comprehensive work on Clergy Sexual Abuse has been helpful for me to understand forgiveness. She writes:

"She needs to be clear – as do others – that forgiveness is no substitute for justice. In fact, forgiveness must include justice as the unfair hurt is recognized. A woman may find that before she can forgive the perpetrator, she must forgive the forces that allowed her to be hurt. If she thinks she had some responsibility for what happened to her, that she somehow allowed herself to be vulnerable, then she must forgive herself. That forgiveness involves admitting her own sense of guilt, confessing it, and accepting the forgiveness of God. She may well need a professional to sort out with her what proportion of responsibility she bore for what happened. Even though she recognizes the abuse of power that took place, she still may have had some agency, however minor it might have been. Taking a thorough inventory of what responsibility she feels for her victimization takes seriously the complexity of causation with which she may be struggling. Forgiveness of the perpetrator may only be able to come after, or at least intertwined with, forgiving herself and seeking and believing in God's forgiveness.

Even more difficult may be forgiving God. How could God have let this happen to her, perhaps in God's very name? It may be very difficult to forgive God, both for the victimization and for the lack of justice that may be her experience with those who should be concerned about justice. The pain inflicted on her in processes of revictimization by the church, either through its minimization or ignoring what happened or through scapegoating and rejecting her, may deepen her anger at God as well as the church. Any process of forgiving the perpetrator needs to take into full account those who allowed him to do this to her—herself, God, the church, and those who perhaps could have protected her if they had acted on what they knew. Recognizing the complexity and arduous work involved in forgiveness is a first step." 14

Further Resources on Clergy Sexual Abuse

YOUTUBE TALK:

<u>Sex with a Pastor is never an Affair</u> by Cameron Altaras
https://www.youtube.com/watch?v=32iVyVVta2s
Dec 15, 2015 - Uploaded by Jeff Altaras
2015 SNAP Conference (Survivors Network of those Abused by Priests) Alexandria, Virginia August 2, 2015

ARTICLES AND STUDIES:

Understanding Sexual Abuse by a Church Leader or Caregiver
(<u>http://mcccanada.ca/media/resources/1340</u>)

"Soul Stealing: Power Relations in Pastoral Sexual Abuse" byPamela Cooper White (Snapnetwork.org)

"Sex In The Forbidden Zone" by Peter Rutter

(https://www.ministrymagazine.org/archive/1992/01/
sex-in-the-forbidden-zone)

"Sexual Sin in the Ministry" by Harry Schaumburg
(http://www.desiringgod.org)

"When Wolves Wear Sheep's Clothing" by Diana
Garland
(http://www.tamarsvoice.org/articles-and-resources.
html)

"Why Adult Victims of Clergy Sexual Abuse are Not
To Blame" by Mark Scheffers
(http://www.tamarsvoice.org/articles-and-resources.
html)

WEBSITES:

Founded by Marie Fortune
www.faithtrustinstitute.org

Seeking an end to clergy sexual abuse
http://predatorypastors.com/home.html

A ministry devoted to survivors of clergy sexual abuse
http://www.thehopeofsurvivors.com

Confronting Collusion with Abuse in the Faith
Community - A great website with lots of information.
www.takecourage.org

Sacred Trust: An educational series on sexual misconduct in the church.
https://mcec.ca/

A website run by a CSA survivor
http://www.survivorsawakenthechurch.com

A website run by survivors
http://www.acryinthechurch.com

Clergy sexual misconduct
http://www.baylor.edu/clergysexualmisconduct/

The Voice of a Clergy Sexual Abuse Survivor
http://sharonsrose.org/

Dispelling Myths about Adult Clergy Sexual Abuse
http://www.educatingtoendabuse.com/id22.html

BLOGS and Personal Stories:

Personal stories http://predatorypastors.com/blog.html

Personal stories http://sharonsrose.org/

BOOKS on Clergy Sexual Abuse:

Responding to Clergy Misconduct: A Handbook. Dr. Marie M. Fortune et al, published by the FaithTrust Institute.(2009) An effective response to clergy sexual abuse will help the victim heal, help the congregation deal with the pastor's betrayal, prevent abuse by holding offenders accountable, and protect the church's resources. This book is an invaluable resource for judicatory leaders and church leaders, and it's also great for survivors.

Is Nothing Sacred? When Sex Invades the Pastoral Relationship. *(1989)* One of the first resources available is still one of the best, Marie Fortune's Is Nothing Sacred? When Sex Invades the Pastoral Relationship (1989). It is a A moving case study of a church and its charismatic "successful" new pastor who, during a four-year pastorate, involved himself sexually with a number of its women members. The circumstances included harassing phone calls in the middle of the night, rape, and seduction of those to whom he had offered care during grief and family crises. Fortune was called upon to offer counsel to and advocacy on behalf of six women who came forward in order to stop their pastor from abusing others. Evidently, there were many more victims who did not speak out. Perhaps the most frightening aspects of the story are the slow and ineffectual responses to the victims of the congregational and denominational leaders. The book provides procedures for responding to clergy sexual abuse, guidance for protecting the clergy person unjustly accused, and approaches for congregations and denominational leaders dealing with such a crisis.

When A Congregation is Betrayed. Beth Ann Gaede, Editor When a Congregation Is Betrayed offers strategic resources to help clergy and lay leaders ultimately to survive and serve well in congregations where clergy misconduct has occurred. Many books, videos, curricula, and organizations address clergy misconduct and its effects on congregations, and the resource section at the end of this volume lists a number of valuable tools recommended by the contributors. In the earliest conversations that led to the development of this book, however, we asked ourselves, "What is missing? What do congregation leaders need to know that no one else has covered?" During many hours of telephone conference calls held over the course of about a year, it became clear we were being called to write a book that focuses on misconduct by clergy involving adult victims.

Victim to Survivor. by Nancy Poling
Following powerful introductions by Marie Fortune and by the editor, women tell their actual stories of being victimized by religious leaders and how they have survived. Victims can find themselves and their experiences in these stories and not feel so alone.

Sexual abuse of Women by Members of the Clergy. by Kathryn Flynn
The sexual abuse and exploitation of women by members of the clergy is not a new issue. What is new is the public's growing understanding of what is involved when members of the clergy ignore or repeatedly fall short of legal and ethical requirements to adhere to the expected standards of conduct. This work is based on the author's study of 25 women from 11 states who were sexually abused by members of the clergy. A primary goal of the study was to help the violated women understand their experiences and

make available to educators, practitioners and others concrete information about what it means to be sexually exploited by a trusted religious representative. The author also considers the viability of a trauma model to study the impact of such sexual abuse on women and on their relationships with others, and presents her findings that the participants did exhibit symptoms that strongly correspond with the classical and complex trauma criteria used.

Sex in the Forbidden Zone: When Men in Power Betray Women's Trust. by Dr. Peter Rutter
A psychiatrist, Rutter provides case studies of men in power—therapists, doctors, clergy, teachers, mentors—who betrayed women's trust by involving them sexually.

How Little We Knew: Collusion and Confusion with Sexual Misconduct. by Dee Ann Miller
Whistleblowers in the institutional church seldom find honor from the system. Neither did this author from the beginning. Both she and her husband were "rewarded" for speaking the truth about a sexual predator-colleague by disillusionment and career derailments in 1988 because they had refused to stop confronting the same monstrous organization that was protecting the perpetrator with hand-slapping gestures. To make matters worse, this all occurred in Africa-yes on the mission field with a young national and another

teenager among the victims! When given a choice between keeping their careers or keeping their voices, the couple found the courage to choose the latter.

Enlarging Boston's Spotlight: A Call for Courage, Integrity, and Institutional Integrity. By Dee Ann Miller

Enlarging Boston's Spotlight, is a first-person, eye-witness account of a little-known aspect of activism that occurred years before Boston Globe Spotlight journalists became actively involved to expose the institutional church's entrenched, secretive approach, in all forms of abuse, on many levels. It's filled with dramatic moments, interspersing years of waiting and hoping that goes on to this day, often forcing survivors and their advocates to work underground in order to survive and find spiritual freedom in the process.

Yet the book goes far beyond this topic. It spills out into the larger society, offering tips and insights into the reasons for complicity, by showing the importance of connections, and the role of advocates and activists who are willing to take on the resistance to change in our institutions and throughout our world so torn apart by oppression and violence.

Betrayal of Trust: Confronting and Preventing Clergy Sexual Misconduct. by Stanley Grenz and Roy Bell

Sexual misconduct by clergy is a devastating issue that reaches across all denominations, damaging the credibility of the church in its wake. The media regularly reports on the moral failure of leaders and abuse at the hands of those who are supposed to be trustworthy.

Questions & Answers about Clergy Sexual Misconduct. (from the Interfaith Sexual Trauma Institute) by Dr. Elizabeth Horst

When Pastors Prey. by Valli Boobal Batchelor
This book gathers essays from familiar U.S. leaders like Jimmy Carter, Diana Garland, Marie Fortune, Martin Weber, Pamela Cooper-White, and Samantha Nelson, along with an astounding collection of voices of survivors and advocates from Africa, Southeast Asia, Europe, and Australia. Clergy sexual abuse is a worldwide problem, and this book brings leaders together for a worldwide response.

EXAMPLES of DENOMINATIONAL POLICIES:

- The Community Christian Fellowship Church of Canada

Clergy Sexual Misconduct Policy

- Anglican Church of Canada Diocese of Toronto

Sexual Misconduct Policy: Sexual Harassment, Exploitation and Assault. October 2001; Revised February, 2004. Click here for full forty page policy (pdf file).

Sexual exploitation is any form of sexual contact or invitation to sexual contact with an adult by a professional person, cleric or anyone in a position of authority, trust or power over that adult whether or not there is consent from the individual ... Meaningful consent for sexual activity is not possible in a fiduciary relationship.

- <u>Anglican Church Diocese of Sydney Australia</u> (nine page pdf document)

Sexual misconduct is inappropriate sexual behaviour towards an adult by a church worker where that behaviour would constitute a criminal offence or an abuse of a pastoral relationship.

- <u>Baptist General Convention of Texas, Christian Life Commission</u>

Ministerial Ethics: A Covenant of Trust. Part VII. Sexual Conduct.

One of the most destructive moral failures by clergy is sexual misconduct. The damage caused by this failure spreads like a virus throughout the church, devastating families and individuals. Sexual failures are often headline news, implicating clergy in all religious bodies.

In one study questionnaires were sent to 1000 Baptist pastors. Of those responding, 14.1 percent acknowledged inappropriate sexual contact in their ministries; 70.4 percent said they knew of some other minister's sexual failings; and 24.2 percent reported that they had counseled at least one person who claimed to have had sexual contact with a minister.

- <u>Evangelical Lutheran Church of America.</u>

Safe Connections: What Parishioners Can Do to Understand and Prevent Clergy Sexual Abuse.

What is clergy sexual abuse? Clergy sexual abuse is a boundary violation. Sexual activity in the context of a relationship between parishioner and pastor is an improper and harmful use of that relationship. Clergy sexual abuse violates the sacred purpose of the pastoral relationship.

- Evangelical Lutheran Church in Canada.

Sexual Abuse or Harassment Policy, March 2006.

… it is stressed that where one person holds power over another, either in fact or perceived, a relationship of mutual consent may be impossible to achieve …

It is inappropriate for a rostered minister to date a parishioner or someone working under the minister's supervision within the congregation he or she is serving, until that relationship has ceased for a period of at least one year and after consultation with the synod bishop.

- Mennonite Central Committee.

Professional Misconduct: What is Professional/ Clergy Misconduct?

Professional/Clergy misconduct is a violation of professional ethics, a violation of personal boundaries, a violation of trust and power. Where an imbalance of power exists, there can be no authentic consensual relationship.

Marie Fortune describes the emotional cost of such violations for the victims including feelings of shame, guilt, stupidity, betrayal, and exploitation. The victims become depressed and lose faith in themselves and their religious convictions …

Clergy misconduct is a grave injustice toward another person and an entire religious community. It is a power issue. A sacred trust is violated.

- Presbyterian Church of the US.

Creating Safe Churches.

While sexual misconduct is not limited to clergy, research indicates that between 10 and 23 percent of clergy (of all faiths) have engaged in inappropriate sexual behavior with church members, clients or employees with whom they have a professional relationship.

Because a fiduciary relationship is based on authority, trust and power, it renders sexual misconduct inappropriate and wrong.

- Roman Catholic Diocese of Oakland

No More Secrets, Survivors of Clergy Sexual Abuse. (oakdiocese.org/survivors/inside.pdf)

Can clergy sexual activity ever be consensual on the part of the victim?

NEVER! The power differential in the relationship automatically puts the priest (or deacon) in the position of power. Therefore, there can never exist a true mutually consensual agreement. It is the obligation of the priest (or clergy) to hold the sexual boundaries in all relationships.

- <u>United Methodist, General Commission on the Status and Role of Women</u>

Sexual Ethics Welcome Page.

It's about power ... Clergy misconduct of a sexual nature (clergy sexual misconduct) is about power—power which is abused through sexualized behavior. It is always the PASTOR'S responsibility to ensure that appropriate boundaries are experienced in the pastor-congregant relationship ...

Please note that this website is about clergy misconduct of a sexual nature which happens between adults and is not about child sexual abuse ... We understand that sexual abuse can occur in many different relationships, however, this resource addresses the specific dynamics of the pastor/parishioner relationship.

<u>**Definition of Consent**</u> as listed in section 273.1 of the criminal code of Canada:

(2) No consent is obtained, for the purposes of sections 271, 272 and 273, where

(a) the agreement is expressed by the words or conduct of a person other than the complainant;

(b) the complainant is incapable of consenting to the activity;

(c) the accused induces the complainant to engage in the activity by abusing a position of trust, power or authority;

(d) the complainant expresses, by words or conduct, a lack of agreement to engage in the activity; or

(e) the complainant, having consented to engage in sexual activity, expresses, by words or conduct, a lack of agreement to continue to engage in the activity.

(c) the accused induces the complainant to engage in the activity by abusing a position of trust,

ACKNOWLEDGEMENTS

WHEN I THINK OF THE PEOPLE GOD PUT INTO MY LIFE to hold me up during the darkest times, I think of my family. The word "steadfast" comes to mind when I think of my mom. She was my anchor when I was dazed and confused. She was my guide when I nearly lost my way in the darkness of what had actually happened to me versus the story everyone was told. Thank you, Mom, for bravely standing by my side and experiencing with me the revictimization as I told my story over and over again. I think of my Dad who also took a stand for truth and paid a high price. Thank you, Dad, for being a Truth Teller no matter what the cost!

I think of my brother, Shawn, who was reading a document my mom wrote to try and explain to the denomination what had really happened. When he told me he started weeping at page 6 and couldn't continue, I realized again how lucky I am to have him as my big brother. I think of my children who literally forced me out of bed every day when I just wanted to disappear forever. They also paid a dear price as their entire little communities were ripped away from them. Even though they didn't understand what was happening, I knew their little hearts were hurting for me.

And I think of a handful of dear friends who wouldn't let me go. My "security detail" when we would go shopping! Tim Horton's coffee being dropped off at random hours! And dear, dear Gaby, who was so afraid to betray my confidence but in reality, saved my life. And there were others, like David Ratray, who were not afraid to speak truth.

I think of Tim Callaway and Elsie Goerzen, who became pillars of strength and encouragement and fellow truth bearers for us. Tim, your humor and your great big heart are a safe place for me and many others. And Elsie, I can't forget how you hit the dashboard of the car with your hand as you said, "It was not a confession! It was a disclosure!!" as I was recounting how I had "confessed" what happened. You gave me courage to acknowledge the truth.

And Steve Masterson, you have not only counseled us through strongholds and symptoms of PTSD, but you've become a mentor and friend and "Jesus with skin on" to us. I am so grateful for you and Jackie.

And finally, I'm so thankful for my husband. Right from the beginning, when you were as confused as I was, you turned to Jesus like never before. You prayed when I couldn't. You held me up when I couldn't stand on my own. You loved me when everything I thought I was had been stripped away and torn into shreds. You have laid your hands on my head and prayed protection over my mind and against flashbacks and nightmares. And you have rejoiced so deeply with me as God has restored and renewed what was stolen and mangled.

Words do not adequately express what the Body of Christ has meant to me!

I remember Steve telling me that when I start singing again, God would make a spectacle of the enemy and evil would have to admit defeat. Only God could have choreographed this story – and I look forward to the rest of the story He's planning to write!

Kristal Chalmers

NOTES

Chapter 1 What Is Clergy Sexual Abuse?

1. Beth Ann Gaede, Editor, When A Congregation Is Betrayed: Responding to Clergy Misconduct. (Rowman & Littlefield Publishers, 2005) 75.

2. Peter Rutter, Sex in the Forbidden Zone. (New York: Fawcett Columbine, 1989).

3. Gaede, When A Congregation Is Betrayed, 17.

4. United Methodist Church, 2004 Book of Resolutions, General Commission on the Status and Role of Women, 151.

Chapter 2 Groomed For Abuse

5. Mennonite Central Committee U.S. "Understanding sexual abuse by a church leader or caregiver." (2nd edition. 2016). 9

6. Diana Garland "When Wolves Wear Shepherd's Clothing: Helping Women Survive Clergy Sexual Abuse." Social Work & Christianity, Vol. 33, No. 1 (2006), Journal of the North American Association of Christians in Social Work. 7-9

Chapter 3 Understanding Power

7. Dee Ann Miller, "Confronting Collusion With Abuse In The Faith Community." http://www.take-courage.org

8. Garland, "When Wolves Wear Shepherd's Clothing: Helping Women Survive Clergy Sexual Abuse" Social Work & Christianity, 3.

Chapter 4 Soul Stealing

9. Stanley J. Grenz and Roy D. Bell, Betrayal of Trust: Confronting and Preventing Clergy Sexual Misconduct, (Baker Publishing Group; 2 edition Dec 29, 2008) 93

10. Mark Scheffers, "Why Adult Victims of Clergy Sexual Abuse Are Not To Blame", Child Trauma Assessment Center, Western Michigan University. As cited in www.tamarsvoice.org/articles.htm

Chapter 5 Shame and Trauma

11. Nancy Poling, Victim to Survivor; Women Recovering from Clergy Sexual Abuse. (Pilgrim Press, 1999) 99.

12. Wanda Lott Collins "Silent Sufferers: Female Clergy Sexual Abuse", Family and Community Ministries 23 (2009) 10.

Chapter 6 The Healing Power of Grief

13. Ed Batista (quoting Joseph Ledoux), The Value of Journal Writing. (Blog) http://www.edbatista.com2008

Chapter 8 Helping Victims of Clergy Sexual Abuse

14. Garland "When Wolves Wear Shepherd's Clothing: Helping Women Survive Clergy Sexual Abuse." 27,28

Printed in Canada